THE SONG HEARD 'ROUND THE WORLD

A CANTATA FOR CHRISTMAS

BY JOSEPH M. MARTIN

ORCHESTRATIONS BY BRANT ADAMS AND STAN PETHEL

(1) This symbol indicates a track number on the StudioTrax CD (accompaniment only) or SplitTrax CD.

Performance Time: ca. 50 Minutes

ISBN 9-781-4950-9199-5

SHAWNEE PRESS

EXCLUSIVELY DISTRIBUTED BY

HAL•LEONARD®

7777 W. BLUEMOUND RD. P.O. BOX 13819 MILWAUKEE, WI 53213

Visit Hal Leonard Online at
www.halleonard.com/church

Visit Shawnee Press Online at
www.shawneepress.com

THE SONG HEARD 'ROUND THE WORLD

FOREWORD

Let all the world in every corner sing! This is a season for music and celebration!

No other time of the year generates such spiritual devotion. No other festival inspires such sacred adoration. Christmas swirls about us with sounds and songs that gracefully speak to our deepest hopes and dreams. Christmas surrounds the world in a sonic embrace, resonating in us treasured memories of family and faith. It arouses the winter from its frozen sadness and invites our hardened hearts to a divine dance of joy.

Every culture in the world has its own Christmas legacy of song. Wherever there is Christian worship, the eternal story of the holy family is decorated with a lavish diversity of tuneful praise. From intimate lullabies to angelic acclamations, the music of Christmas covers the earth with its message of love and peace.

Now, at a time in our history when diversity has become division, we once again travel together the well-worn path to Bethlehem. As in ancient times, the air is still cluttered with a cacophony of hostile voices, the road jumbled with political dispute and philosophical quarrels. The inns are full and bursting with frustrated pilgrims desperately seeking sanctuary, and the world's earnest prayers for peace are overwhelmed by calls to violence.

Then, breaking through the night comes a still small voice. It floats upon the wind in a delicate nocturne of comfort and assurance. Its gentleness silences the noise and calms the din of murmuring doubt. It breathes stillness into the shadows and falls tenderly upon the wounded and the weary.

The world, now hushed, strains to hear the fragile cry of a newborn baby. Rising like a prayer, a fresh new song goes forth with healing for the nations. At the sound of its heavenly theme, the tragedy of war becomes a tapestry of peace and the dissonance of hate becomes divine harmony.

And so we sing, joining our hearts to the song everlasting. Softly, we begin the music of miracles. Then, encouraged by grace, we lift one mighty voice in a new carol! Christ is born! Glory to God in the highest! Live in heavenly peace!

PROGRAM NOTES

THE SONG HEARD 'ROUND THE WORLD is a cantata that expresses the paradox of diversity and unity. It displays the many varieties of song and worship found throughout the cultures of the world, while celebrating the unity we have in the gospel of Christ. There are many ways in which to display this core principle in your presentation of this work.

Consider a processional of flags representing the national heritages of your congregation. This can take place during the opening movement. The flags can be placed around the sanctuary, or smaller flags can be processed by children and arranged around the front of the church, or placed upon the altar.

Another option is simply to adorn the sanctuary with a colorful array of flags and banners representing some of the areas where your individual church sponsors mission activity.

Feel free to use different languages during the narration time, with the English translation being read after each line for clarity. The more diversity the better!

Feel free to insert other countries and their carols to more accurately reflect your own congregation's national origins. This can be done by using the children's choirs, congregational singing, or solos chosen to reflect these unique characteristics.

Another colorful option is to have the choir dress in traditional festive costumes from their own heritage.

The final movement, "PRAYER FOR PEACE," allows for a traditional "SILENT NIGHT" moment. The extended instrumental interlude is given to allow time for the lighting of candles and the encircling of the congregation by the choir. These ideas can be altered and customized at the discretion of the director.

To take the cantata "beyond the walls," consider providing a time of fellowship following the performance. Set up a diversity of booths where members can provide desserts and baked goods from various countries. Children and adults can dress in traditional costumes and play festive music from the represented countries. This time can be a teachable moment about the wonderful variety of the world's cultures.

Lastly, consider collecting a world missions offering as an act of worship for the cantata event. This can help connect the choir and audience around the themes of artistry, ministry, and community.

These are merely suggestions on extra-musical elements that can be incorporated into your performance. You are encouraged to use your own creativity in adapting the work to meet the specific need of your church and its peoples.

A JOYFUL JOURNEY OF CAROLS

Original Words by
JOSEPH M. MARTIN (BMI)

Traditional Carols
Arranged by
JOSEPH M. MARTIN

With abundant joy (♩ = ca. 96)

ACCOMP.

SOPRANO

*Bring joy! Bring

ALTO

*Bring joy! Bring

TENOR

*Bring joy! Bring

BASS

*Bring joy! Bring

* BRING JOY! - Words and Music by Joseph M. Martin

THE SONG HEARD 'ROUND THE WORLD - SATB

8

* Tune: ANTIOCH, George Frederick Handel, 1685-1759
  Words: Isaac Watts, 1674-1748

THE SONG HEARD 'ROUND THE WORLD - SATB

heav'n and na - ture _ sing, and _ heav'n, _ and heav'n _____ and na - ture

sing.

lightly, gracefully

10

Let all the earth break

praise and lift your voic-es.

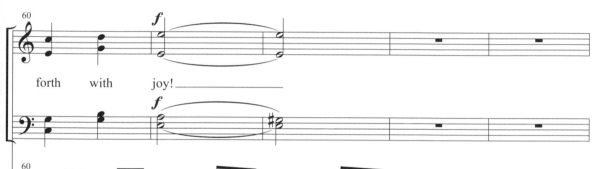

forth with joy!

Like a Celtic jig ($\,.$ = ca. 104)

71

12

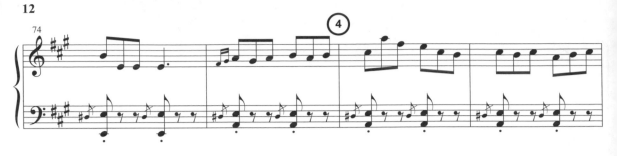

SOPRANO
ALTO

A - rise and shine. Your Light will come on

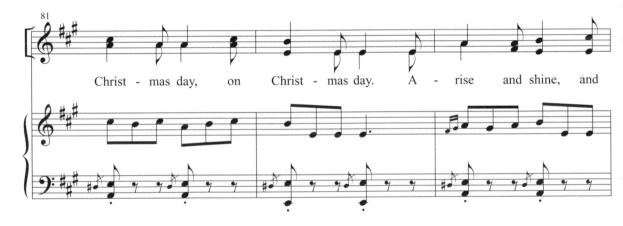

Christ - mas day, on Christ - mas day. A - rise and shine, and

greet the Son on Christ - mas day in the morn - ing.

unis.

TENOR
BASS

Re -

* Tune: traditional English melody
   Words: Joseph M. Martin

THE SONG HEARD 'ROUND THE WORLD - SATB

SOPRANO / ALTO

Un - to us a Child is____ born: Christ, the____ Lord.

* Tune: ROCKING, traditional Czech melody
Words: Joseph M. Martin

THE SONG HEARD 'ROUND THE WORLD - SATB

joy a - bound - ing. An - gels soon will soar on __ high. Glo - ri - a! All __ the __ world in joy __ re - ply.

Rise and __

Rise and __ shine!

* Tune: KOMMET, IHR HIRTEN, traditional Bohemian folk melody
Words: Joseph M. Martin

THE SONG HEARD 'ROUND THE WORLD - SATB

Joyfully, dance-like (♩ = ca. 112)

Un-to us a Son is giv-en. To us a Child is born.

Sing ho - san - na. To us a Child is born.

He shall rule in peace for - ev - er. Zi - on will be re-stored.

Sing ho - san - na. Zi - on will be re-stored.

* Tune: traditional Hebrew folk melody
Words: Joseph M. Martin

THE SONG HEARD 'ROUND THE WORLD - SATB

He shall rule in peace for - ev - er. He will be Lord of lords!

Sing ho - san - na. He will be Lord of lords!

Glo - Glo - ri - a! Glo - ri - a!

Glo - ri - a! Glo - ri - a!

- - ri - a! In ex - cel - sis

Glo - ri - a! Glo - ri - a!

* Tune: GLORIA, traditional French melody
Words: traditional French carol

THE SONG HEARD 'ROUND THE WORLD - SATB

183 With an "islands" feel (♩ = ca. 116)

De - o.

185 ⑨ * **mf** unis.

The

189 vir - gin Ma - ry had a ba - by boy. ___ The vir - gin Ma - ry had a

* Tune: traditional West Indies melody
Words: traditional West Indies carol

THE SONG HEARD 'ROUND THE WORLD - SATB

ba - by boy.___ The vir - gin Ma - ry had a ba - by boy;___ and they

say that His name was Je - sus.___ He come___ from the

glo - ry.___ He come___ from the glo - ri - ous king - dom.

He come_ from the glo - ry.__ He come_ from the glo - ri - ous king - dom. He come_ from the glo - ri - ous king - dom. He come_ from the glo - ri - ous king-dom, the glo-rious king - dom.

* Tune: East African worship song
Words: Joseph M. Martin

THE SONG HEARD 'ROUND THE WORLD - SATB

Lamb. Sing hal - le - lu - jah! Re - joice, all you chil-dren of the Lamb!

239 With great celebration (♩ = ca. 104)

Joy to the earth! The Sav - ior___ reigns. Let choirs their songs em -

239 With great celebration (♩ = ca. 104)

NARRATOR:

Let all the world in every corner sing! This is a time for singing and celebration. This is the season of praise and rejoicing. Everywhere, people are gathering to declare the glory of God and the birth of Jesus, the LIGHT OF THE WORLD; Jesus, the PRINCE OF PEACE. From the east to the west, from the north to the south, let there be music, let there be praise!

HEAR THE SONG HEARD 'ROUND THE WORLD

Words by
JOSEPH M. MARTIN (BMI)

Traditional Catalonian Melody
Arranged by
JOSEPH M. MARTIN

Lightly, with grace (♩ = ca. 132)

ACCOMP.

SOPRANO / ALTO

Hear the song heard 'round the world, 'cross the heav - ens ring - ing. Soon a Child of roy - al birth will

set the earth to sing - ing.

Ev - 'ry heart pre - pare__ the__ way. This could be our

T.B. *p unis.*

danc - ing day. Let the peo - ple sing.

Let the

Re - joice, re - joice with mu - sic;
stee - ples ring. Re - joice, re - joice with mu - sic;

won - drous, glo - rious mu - sic.

Slower, with freedom (♩ = ca. 108)

(Accompanist may double voices, if desired.)

See the glow of dis - tant light. Lo, a star is beam - ing;

shin - ing in the sol - emn night, all the world re - deem - ing.

By its fire the world is healed. God's great glo - ry is re - vealed.

Tempo I (♩ = ca. 132)

Let the can - dles shine Re -

with a Light di - vine.

joice, re - joice with mu - sic; won - drous, glo - rious mu - sic.

Re - joice with mu - sic; won - drous, glo - rious mu - sic.

NARRATOR:

For years, the world waited in darkness for Emmanuel to come. When would God shine His holy light into the shadows of our broken world? Each year, we recall these prayers as we trace their journey of hope and see it reflecting in our own faith story.

Lord, we pray and wait; longing for Your season of grace. In You alone we will rest our hopes and dreams; and upon Your divine promises we place our trust. Come, Emmanuel, come! Come into our hearts and light Your candles of hope, peace, love, and joy. Hear our prayer, O Lord. Hear our prayer.

AN ADVENT PRAYER

Words by
JOSEPH M. MARTIN (BMI)
Incorporating
"O Come, O Come, Emmanuel"
Latin Hymn
tr. by JOHN MASON NEALE (1818-1866)

Traditional Russian Melody (16th c.)
Arranged by
JOSEPH M. MARTIN

* Tune: VENI EMMANUEL, 15th c. plainsong

THE SONG HEARD 'ROUND THE WORLD - SATB

THE SONG HEARD 'ROUND THE WORLD - SATB

ve - ni, ve - ni. We are long - ing for the Light!

man - u - el.

Make us all one heart and mind. We are wait - ing.

rejoin section

Lord, have mer - cy. We are pray - ing in the night.

NARRATOR:

The world prepares for the Christmas season with a rainbow of beautiful traditions. Each culture has its own music, food, and sacred ceremonies that represent the treasured gifts that are the heart of this special time. With rich adornments and sparkling trees, with dazzling lights and festive music, the world celebrates! Yet, it is our hearts that must truly be prepared to receive the gift of Messiah. We must clear away the sin and earthly distractions that separate us from abundant life and joy. All over the world, let every heart prepare Him a room, and make straight the path. Let the valleys be exalted. Let the mountains be brought low. Let the crooked places be straightened and the rough places made plain. Jesus is coming soon. Prepare the way!

PREPARE THE WAY OF THE KING

Words by
JOSEPH M. MARTIN (BMI)

Tune: **GLOUCESTERSHIRE**
Traditional English Melody
Arranged by
JOSEPH M. MARTIN

THE SONG HEARD 'ROUND THE WORLD - SATB

54

THE SONG HEARD 'ROUND THE WORLD - SATB

56

Love and Light are com-ing to you; for Love and Light are com - ing. Pre-pare ye the way. Pre-pare ye the way. Pre-pare ye the way of the King!

Pre-pare ye the way. Pre-pare ye the way, the way of the King!

NARRATOR:
All over the world, the timeless story of Jesus' birth is shared; animated by music from many different languages and traditions. Each time the story is shared it becomes more precious, and with each re-telling, it pushes its graceful truths deeper into our hearts. Hear this account from the book of Matthew:

Now the birth of Jesus the Messiah took place in this way. When his mother Mary had been engaged to Joseph, but before they lived together, she was found to be with child from the Holy Spirit. Her husband Joseph, being a righteous man and unwilling to expose her to public disgrace, planned to dismiss her quietly. But just when he had resolved to do this, an angel of the Lord appeared to him in a dream and said, "Joseph, son of David, do not be afraid to take Mary as your wife, for the child conceived in her is from the Holy Spirit. She will bear a son, and you are to name him Jesus, for he will save his people from their sins." *(Matthew 1:18-21 – NRSV*)*

GESÙ BAMBINO

Words by
FREDERICK H. MARTENS (1874-1932)

Music by
PIETRO YON (1886-1943)
Arranged by
JOSEPH M. MARTIN (BMI)

13 **More quickly, with a lilting motion** (♩. = ca. 58)

(opt. children's choir or soloist)

13 **More quickly, with a lilting motion** (♩. = ca. 58)

O come, let us a - dore Him. O come, let us a - dore Him. O come, let us a -

Ve - ni - te a - do - re - mus. Ve - ni - te a - do - re - mus. Ve - ni - te a - do -

* Tune: ADESTE FIDELES, John Francis Wade, 1711-1786

   Words: Latin hymn, ascribed to John Francis Wade

** Optional Latin text.

THE SONG HEARD 'ROUND THE WORLD - SATB

come, let us a - dore_____ Him._____ Let

gave_____ the world_____ its Christ - mas Rose, its King_____ of love_____ and light._____

swell._____

ev - 'ry voice_____ ac-claim His name. The grate - ful cho - rus swell, the grate - ful

cho - rus swell. From par - a-dise_____ to earth He came that we,_____with Him,_____ might

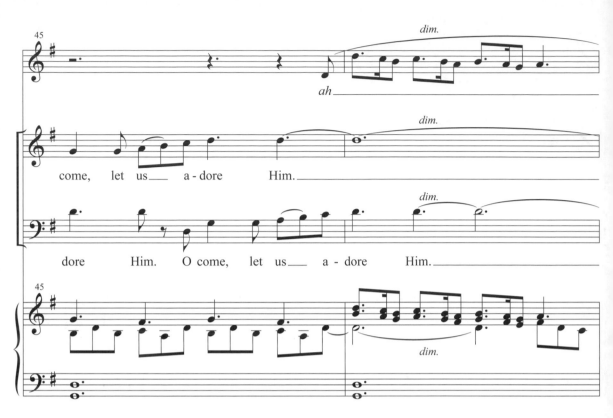

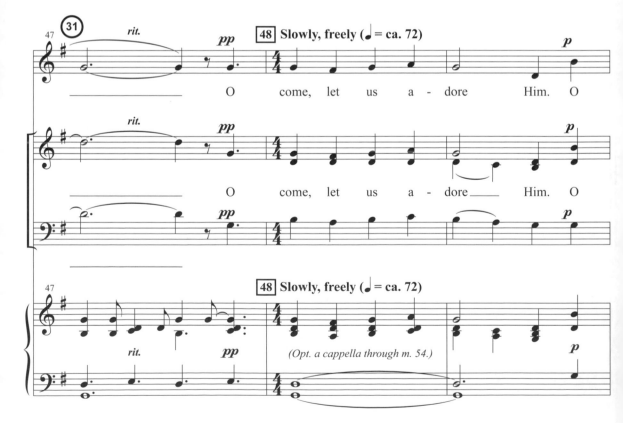

NARRATOR:
The angels declared the birth of the Christ Child with heavenly power. Yet, it was not to the powerful that the message was gifted. The divine declaration was delivered to simple shepherds keeping watch over flocks in the Judean countryside. It was clear from this graceful gesture that this good news was for every person and every nation.

Such magnificent words the angels spoke that night; beautiful words of worship and adoration. And shining brightly in their soaring anthem of praise were the cherished words that we still cling to today: "PEACE ON EARTH."

Such hope and promise these words awaken in us. Why do the nations so furiously rage against one another when, in truth, we are all children of the Light and one people in the promise? Let us then, as one, follow the shepherds to Bethlehem to worship the newborn PRINCE OF PEACE. Together, let us rejoice, for Christ, the Lord, is born!

REJOICE! CHRIST IS BORN!

Words by
JONATHAN MARTIN (ASCAP)

Traditional Finnish Folk Melody
Arranged by
JOSEPH M. MARTIN (BMI)

70

THE SONG HEARD 'ROUND THE WORLD - SATB

72

THE SONG HEARD 'ROUND THE WORLD - SATB

74

Sing un-to the Lord with joy-ful noise! Bring un-to the Lord a

tune-ful voice! Ring the news. Let the world re - joice! Re-

Pm   pm   ti - ki - ti - ki pm   Re-

joice, for Christ is born!

joice, for Christ is born!

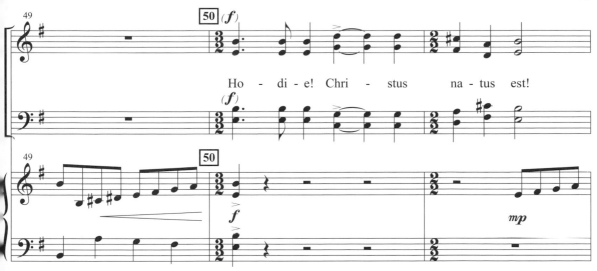

76

78

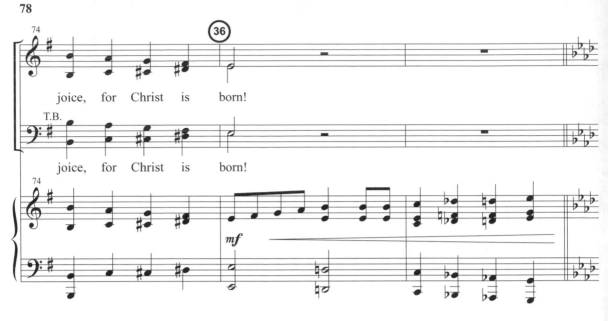

joice, for Christ is born!

T.B.
joice, for Christ is born!

Glo - ry be to___ God on high. Let all cre - a - tion

now re - ply. Lift your voic - es___ to the sky. Re -

THE SONG HEARD 'ROUND THE WORLD - SATB

joice, for Christ is born! Sing un - to the Lord with

joy - ful noise! Bring un - to the Lord a tune - ful voice!

Ring the news. Let the world re - joice! Re - joice, for Christ, the

THE SONG HEARD 'ROUND THE WORLD - SATB

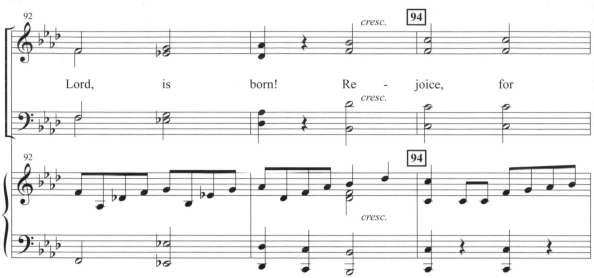

Lord, is born! Re - joice, for

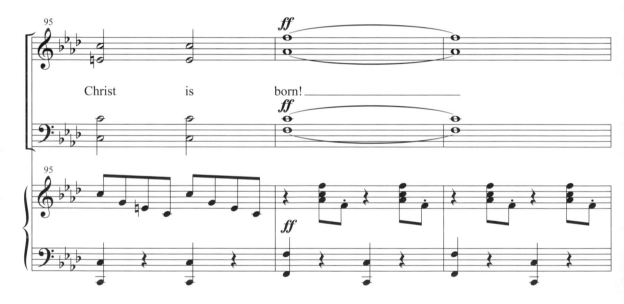

Christ is born!

NARRATOR:

In the days following the birth of Jesus, Magi from the East were led to seek the Holy Child. By placing a star in the sky, it was assured that all could behold the miracle of this sacred moment. These visitors were filled with wisdom, and understood the significance of this moment in time. The wisemen brought gifts to honor Jesus; and still today, throughout the world, their faithfulness is remembered. Like those pilgrims of old, let us unite our hearts together and seek the Peace Child. Let us once again allow the sacred star, that shines forever in the night, to remind us all that we are all children of the light.

for the Westlake UMC Chancel Choir, Austin, Texas,
in celebration of the life of Hortensia R. Sanchez

A UNITY CAROL

Words by
JOSEPH M. MARTIN (BMI)
Incorporating
"In Christ There Is No East or West," *alt.*
by JOHN OXENHAM (1852-1941)

Music by
JOSEPH M. MARTIN
Incorporating
Traditional Brazilian Carol

THE SONG HEARD 'ROUND THE WORLD - SATB

THE SONG HEARD 'ROUND THE WORLD - SATB

We are one in Christ. We are all God's

chil - dren.___ Though we are man - y, we___ are

one in love's___ em - brace. We sing one

song, one "al - le - lu - ia;"

and with one voice of praise, we cel - e - brate God's

grace. Al - le - lu - ia! San - to! San - to! San - to!

HANDCLAPS

(♪ = ♪ throughout)

THE SONG HEARD 'ROUND THE WORLD - SATB

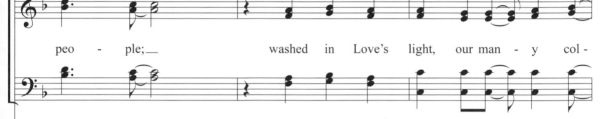

We are one in Christ. We are all one peo - ple;__ washed in Love's light, our man - y col - ors shine as bright as day.__ We have one

NARRATOR:

"In Christ there is no East or West, in Him no South or North; but one great fellowship of love throughout the whole wide earth."* These words call us to consider all the ways we are brought together in the bonds of our shared faith. All of us are unique individuals designed by creator God, redeemed by the grace of Jesus, and brought into unity by the Holy Spirit. In Christ, we have communion, and the dream of peace becomes a shining star of promise in even the darkest night. Although we are many voices, we are but one song singing our praise in glorious harmony to our Savior: the Bright and Morning Star; Jesus, the Light of the world!

* Words by John Oxenham, 1852-1941

MUSIC OF THE MORNING STAR

Words by
JOSEPH M. MARTIN (BMI)

Tunes: **SIYAHAMBA,**
AFRICAN NOEL
and **KUM BA YAH**
Arranged by
JOSEPH M. MARTIN

* Tune: SIYAHAMBA, traditional South African folk melody

THE SONG HEARD 'ROUND THE WORLD - SATB

lu - i - a!__ O we are mu-sic of the Morn-ing Star.__ We are

lu - i - a!__ O we are mu-sic of the Morn-ing Star.__ We are

mu-sic of the Morn-ing Star.__

mu-sic of the Morn-ing Star.__

(end solo)

96

* Tune: AFRICAN NOEL, traditional African folk melody
Words: traditional African carol

THE SONG HEARD 'ROUND THE WORLD - SATB

unis.

peace._____ O Lord,_____

Sing we all No - el.

cresc. poco a poco   *(end opt. children's choir)*

teach us peace._____

cresc. poco a poco

cresc. poco a poco

48

poco rit.

In_____ this_____

poco rit.

THE SONG HEARD 'ROUND THE WORLD - SATB

NARRATOR:

And now, receive this final blessing as we prepare to go into the world and share the light of Christ.

Creator God, giver of every good and perfect gift, thank You for sending Your everlasting Light into the world. Help us always to keep the joy of Christmas deep in our hearts, so that we might know the wonder of this season in all of its abundance.

May we all begin the work of Christmas in our hearts and in our homes. May we carry the peace and love of Christ into all of the world. May God's great grace shine like a brilliant star in every land, and may our hope and prayer now and everyday, be, "Let there be peace on earth."

(You may use different speakers and include other languages as you desire.)

Let there be peace…
Paz	(Spain)
Salim	(Arabia)
Paix	(France)
Pace	(Italy)
Perdamaian	(Indonesia)
Mir	(Russia)
Freda	(Germany)
Pyeonghwa	(Korea)
Ukuthula	(Zulu)
Shalom	(Israel)
Shanti	(India)
Dohiyi	(Native American Cherokee)
Amani	(Swahili)
Maluhia	(Hawaii)
Eirene	(Greece)

Peace…Peace on earth!

Let us now all light the candle of peace, and remember that the light still shines in the darkness, and the darkness has not overcome it.

PRAYER FOR PEACE

Tunes: **WHOLE WORLD,**
DONA NOBIS PACEM,
and **STILLE NACHT**
Arranged by
JOSEPH M. MARTIN (BMI)

* Tune: WHOLE WORLD, traditional spiritual

THE SONG HEARD 'ROUND THE WORLD - SATB

SOPRANO / ALTO
(opt. solo or children's choir)

31 **Gently flowing** (♩ = ca. 80)

Do - na   no - bis   pa - cem,

* Tune: DONA NOBIS PACEM, traditional
  Words: traditional Latin. Translation: "Grant us peace."

THE SONG HEARD 'ROUND THE WORLD - SATB

110

na   no - bis____ pa - cem.   Do - na

no - bis   pa -   cem.

cresc.

mf

(Divide choir into 3 groups of any voicing.)

52

GROUP 1

64

mp unis.

Do - na   no - bis

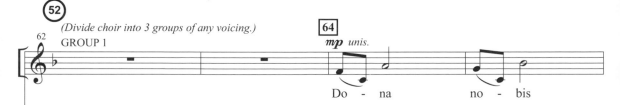

mp

THE SONG HEARD 'ROUND THE WORLD - SATB

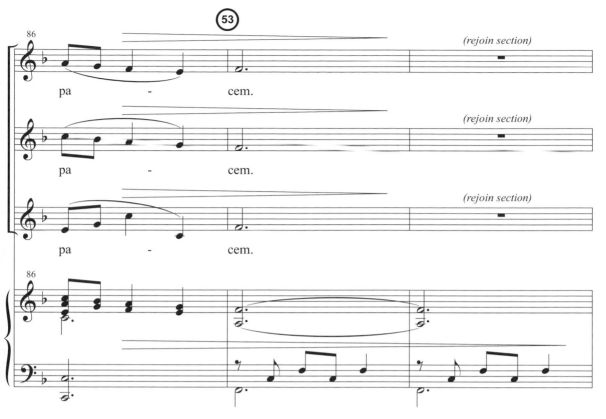

114

*   Part for congregation is on page 119.
** Tune: STILLE NACHT, Franz Grüber, 1787-1863
Words: Joseph Mohr, 1792-1848

THE SONG HEARD 'ROUND THE WORLD - SATB

SILENT NIGHT, HOLY NIGHT

Words:
JOSEPH MOHR (1792-1848)

Tune: **STILLE NACHT**
FRANZ GRÜBER (1787-1863)
Arranged by
JOSEPH M. MARTIN (BMI)